UNCOLLECTED POEMS

Uncollected Poems

Micah Ballard

San Francisco, California

© 2026 Micah Ballard

All rights reserved

ISBN: 979-8-9921594-6-2

Some of these poems have previously appeared in: *Art Fuse, Big Bell #8, The Brooklyn Rail, Spirit Duplicator, Nice Try!, Punks Like Us, Egyptian Magick, Funeral Rites, Ziploc Kids, Imaginary Friendships, Tramp Like Me, Mars Occultation, A$AP Rocky & Rhianna*, and the book *Angel Dust* (above / ground press), 2025.

Titles from the following artists: "Morning Star" by Cass McCombs; "Roll Up" by GX1000; "Advance Cassette" by Spoon: "Miss World" by Hole; "Xoxo" by Elliot Smith; "Bout it Bout it" by Master P; "Suitcase of Memories" by Cyndi Lauper; "Watch Me Jumpstart" by Guided by Voices, "Some Get Translucent" by Kevin Opstedal, "Many Men" by 50 Cent, and "Live to Tell" by Madonna.

All poems were written between July 28, 2024, to July 28, 2025, between various places, mostly in San Francisco and New Orleans.

Thanks to Lorca Manale Ballard, Sunnylyn Thibodeaux, Patrick James Dunagan, Jeff Butler, Charles Gonzalez, Andrew Schultz, Sarah Cain, Christina Fisher, Gloria Frym, John Coletti, Sarah Menefee, Derek Fenner, Maw Shein Win, Ava Koohbor, Jason Morris, Rod Roland, Gillian Conoley, Norma Cole, Joanne Kyger, Diane di Prima, Kevin Opstedal, Will Yackulic, Xylor Jane, Garrett Caples, Colter Jacobsen, Ryan Newton, Alicia McCarthy, and Gautam Sahi.

Cover artwork by Matt Gonzalez

Author photo by Kellam Eanes

San Francisco, California

CONTENTS

Preface   i

Waller Street	1
Walking Around the Venue	2
Morning Star	3
Cheap & Rich	4
Hello	5
Becoming	6
Ethereal	7
Lower Echelon	8
Forfeiture	9
Lost Tapes	10
Notwithstanding	11
Moreso	12
Roll Up	13
Modular	14
Rose Gold	15
Hop Scotch	16
Randy & Benny	17
Novelette	18
How	19
Used To	20
Inhale at Will	21
Aforementioned	22
Goon Squad	23
Cleo	24
Farmer	25
Insignificant Others	26

Verisimilitude	27
Salvo	28
Calling Card	29
Pendulous	30
Tell Me	31
Ink	32
Via	33
Under Which	34
Hindsight	35
What to Do	36
New Convert	37
Non Sequitur	38
Very Vibrant	39
Proprietary	40
Fanzine Hooks	41
Sunbeamers	42
Kerfuffle	43
In Cahoots	44
C'mon	45
Ist	46
Parallels	47
Blow Darts	48
Live to Tell	49
First Dibs	50
Ask Again	51
Rip Grip	52
Off the Plate	53
On Behalf	54
Memoria	55
Blurting Out	56

Wheel Bite	57
Concussional	58
Vert Button	59
Gnar Jar	60
Pitch Wince	61
Comeback Inn	62
Low Life High Life	63
Tryouts	64
Field Energy	65
Paraphernalia	66
Synonyms	67
Futurama Futuresque	68
Floriography	69
Anxieatic	70
Perfunctory	71
Invisibly Bragging	72
Infomercial	73
Portmanteau	74
Live at the Paramount	75
In Bursts	76
Apprehensional	77
Flaunting	78
About About	79
Insofar Soonish	80
All in All	81
Frontside Hurricanes	82
In as Much	83
Anonymity	84
What About	85
Laid Out	86

Going Rate	87
Nightly	88
Tantrums	89
Unmastered	90
Bayside	91
Maybe Someday	92
Quasi Subsidiary	93
Up in the Air	94
Up to Levels	95
One of the Very	96
All Sorts	97
Angel Dust	98
Taped Speeches	99
Grande Amber	100
Outliving	101
In Other Words	102
Unadmittedly	103
The Waning Hours	104
Twice the Vibes	105
Inside out	106
Pretty Much	107
At the Larchmont	108
Celibacy	109
Advance Cassette	110
Radio Ready	111
Dauntingly	112
Spacing Out	113
Vicarious Cardigan	114
After All	115
Minimum Hype	116

At the Bequest	117
Miss World	118
Plurals	119
Uh Oh	120
Get Me Down	121
Reciprocalities	122
David's Morphine	123
Magick Markers	124
For Realeth	125
Inudated	126
Emmanuel Baptist Church	127
Seem Seemingly	128
Taking a Nap	129
Verifying Vivify	130
Xoxo'd	131
At Any Cost	132
Treasure Island Express	133
All Up in It	134
What Gives	135
Blanketed	136
I Got Five On It	137
Sorta Like	138
Dapperville	139
Vape Heavenal	140
In Affect	141
A Lot of Lore	142
Catching Up	143
Van Ness	144
Cigarette Burns	145
Byzantium	146

Hiding Out	147
In a Pool of Blood	148
Hexing Zesty	149
Silviculture	150
Cold Call	151
Out of Pocket	152
Proof of Concept	153
Bout it Bout it	154
Icing Hands	155
Con / Courteous	156
The Palatial Apartments of Being	157
Bayside Marin	158
Way More Lush	159
Blow Candles Burn Tapes	160
Sometime All the Time	161
Bay Bae	162
High Rise	164
Benecia Smiles	165
Oopstory Retreats	166
Cold Pranking	167
Other Seconds	168
So Sayeth	169
All Agog	170
Uncle Charlie	171
Unusually Usual	172
On Occasion	173
The Uns	174
Game Game	175
Moon Flask	176
Chagrin'd	177

Splicing Tape	178
Suitcase of Memories	179
Gone Gone	180
Crayola	181
Insofar	182
The Jams	183
Faux Eros	184
Getting Validated	185
Profusely	186
So Saith Ye	187
Hey Anne!	188
Subthot	189
The Palms	190
Live at the Metro	191
Watch Me Jumpstart	192
Anonymity	193
Precipitation	194
Whatevs	195
Connoisseurship	196
Green Sealing Wax	197
Chroniques	198
Limbos	199
Mushroom Hieroglyphics	200
Rougarou For You	201
Nothing Noting	202
Carrying a Trance	203
Mia Victoriana	204
Gautam	205
Winn-Dixie	206
Turning Out	207

Take A Hike	208
Ethereal Atributal	209
Tomfoolery	210
Yours or Theirs	211
XV11	212
Some get Translucent	213
Platonical	214

PREFACE

This is a night book, in the sense that most poems were composed in the dark, with little or no light. They are jottings, things that may work out into something without a hand in it. They are chronological with no predetermined order, just how they show up, so are kept that way without editing. What joy and freedom. Some like themselves, others not so much. Cosmological neighbors in multiple neighborhoods of small notebooks. To get to the point, or remember half dreams and where's the pen and paper? Figure out the handwriting later. The cartography reveals itself during and after. Time to wake up and take it easy, see when, where, and how we've traveled.

Micah Ballard
San Francisco, CA

WALLER STREET

Malnourished
I get pumped by In Utero
& show up to the skatepark
limping after icing my ankle from
A frontside disaster
I got interviewed for four hours
& brought tons of strangers
into the situation. Emmy is
teaching children to skate
& had the sickest slappies
I gave her my Cleopatra mirror
caught at Mardi Gras. I caught
Nico's board before it hit the curb
They took pictures of my rose
gold nails and rings. I felt like
Frank Costello in court on camera

WALKING AROUND THE VENUE

No comments
I think I was there wearing a scarf
over my beanie
my sunglasses were breaking
but I still wore them crooked
lots of talking and faux promoting
I pretty much avoided everything
had an anxiety attack
in a sauna at the Hotel Biltmore in Los Angeles
It's supposed be haunted
I asked the janitors about it
that's why I reserved us there
the basement pool
was so cold, the ornamental
atmospherics were amazing
did I see a ghost? Or was it me
traipsing around the halls
looking for something

MORNING STAR

Leave your husband
& come with me. Morning
Star hanging high
Morning star tell no lie
Ring my neck
under your thighs
Hole me up to see your face
What's it like to shoot in space?
Shitty songs, shitty hearts, shitty poems
Morning star illuminate
Free us from this world of hate
Morning star now I see
All your secrets are safe with me

CHEAP & RICH

Relatively unknown
only a few short months
a one-time small-town deadbeat
rock and roll space alien
green grapes and toe nails rosy blue
crappy little stereo
A very short hallway to the bedroom
the smell of jasmine
I instantly finally feel comfortable
& play it cool, while I keep calling you
emails and texts are evidence
back to counting logs in the lumber mill
I sat by the footstool talking
& started asking questions
A theatrically manly voice to exchange smiles
the whole apparatus around me
Hide the bad parts. A risky gamble but canny
I was mostly pretty mediocre
just spacing out for a moment
Is someone goofing me for a payback?
Introduce yourself laser beam eyes
screw all these charismatic people sucking the life
I like high voltage people too
I am one of them
there is no artifice. I mean everything every millisecond
then don't so sorry. Super frustrating
No control to the burn
you partition it in the mind

HELLO

for Joanne Kyger

I have this idea
of consistently reaching some higher region
I might not be a part of it but that's okay
Just trying to get there
Isn't that the work of a poet
Maybe so, maybe not
The gift is that we get to try
Enough of this, did I just fart in yoga?
Can I say that? I always felt free
I still do but it's hard these days. Words
& new navigationals are tricky
So time to stay on top! Can you give me
a call back, no emails please
they keep of track of all that shit

BECOMING

You go thru my bag
wanting to find something
I already hid it even tho it wasn't there
You question about the day or evening
I have both and navigate them quite finely
It's true they are rough and there's something
called responsibility. Robert Duncan
called it a responsibility to glory. Not my case.
Hey, I want all the glory just no hassles
A little bit of appreciation can be nice
Just no hassles and a bit of glory
I'm told they go a long way

ETHEREAL

Criminally
otherwise the mistresses
trade me as they see. Mary
& Brandy. I rob
their gates by touching them
Only the gold *fleur-de-lis*
I touch so many
Surely a gate can carry
the energy?

LOWER ESCHELON

How did
we survive?

I put myself out here
posting my own

footage (poems)
everybody

their own brand now
I come off a different highway

Can we still get
a slide hustle?

FORFEITURE

Naturally
unaffected I move in slides
& slants
you are a part of them
how would you know, you don't
Only I do. We hold this
between us. Without you knowing
without me knowing

LOST TAPES

Nothing relaxes
inaccurate frequencies
dictate the teller
I don't have any money
All my footage is lost
someone has it
check the bookshelves
what's inside books

NOTWITHSTANDING

Scoffed
by everybody
a bunch of knuckle draggers
fronting a stock hardness
anyone with skin in the game
is touting features
in the same neighborhood of performance
All this blather to reveal
a tiny item of product
Discuss among yourselves
after the session I cross streams
introducing amazement
I'll be your guest model
makes sense-ish
talk to the new rippers

MORESO

Chasing this
thing together
where does it come from
the lines never meet up
I make up words because they spell me
No more sleeping
on the floor and writing on my body
In the dark with a magic marker
It feels great
but so does everything
Am I "a feeler"
that sounds cringe
I think it's empathy and joy
for personal relationships
with strangers
you know, people you know
but don't know

ROLL UP

Too many
dimensions, call them up
you never hear back
what you got on it
it may be a different stipulation
Oh that's a nice word
apparently it's a
a condition or requirement
that is specified
or demanded as part of
an agreement. Okay
subservient to the will
I get it, good one. I mostly do
let's just listen to Vampire
on Titus

MODULAR

What
you gonna say
about it all
I don't know either
I hate questions in poems
But c'mon what's the score
What happened
how did it happen
I really don't care who did what
How do you communicate
& how does it feel
to keep trying

ROSE GOLD

I don't want you
to be my favorite
nail polish
you're so hard
to find. When I walk
around I'm stunning
something about
how you match
with my rings
I'm not sure where
they came from
Mother-in-law
I romantized they
were from Sicily
when I look down
on my nails
I think of Dylan
Rieder and Lorca
the rings are all Esther

HOP SCOTCH

No thanks
more than yesterday
what we got on it
I don't care who you are
yes I do I'm so sorry
I'm trying to be commendable
does that mean praiseworthy
Who cares, let's get it
I'm wearing my new BS detector vest
it's all situational
The music runs its course
I don't care about surveillance
a lot of controversy
indicates a lack of sharing
Is this the Bermuda Triangle
now that's a story
the kiss of death
grab rails abbreviating
no one names tricks anymore
tighten my trucks
destroy my bushings

RANDY & BENNY

Randy got out
of prison so did Ben
They were gnarly fighters
Randy threw someone
out of a window in art class
I gave them a little money
& said raid the closet
I got into a boxing match
with Benny in a back yard
There were bets on it
I bet on myself
he was the best drummer
I was the new skater will all the tricks
I broke his board
on a hardflip. He's a good fighter
but I can duck
& give a mean southpaw
with Randy he got me
he hung himself

NOVELETTE

No you didn't
yeah you did, don't front
that's a lot of dungeons and dragons
I'm not sure where I am
we're both on the couch naked
must be the morphine
I think it's mushrooms
did you pocket that heroin Visine bottle
I bought the black tar
on 16th wearing a borrowed
windbreaker to look sketchy
then walked to a block on 24th
A car delivered, we cooked it
It was very numbing
lasted for hours

HOW

Unfortunance
arrives, what to do with it
does it own me
or can I shed it off quick
may take a little bit
that's okay I'm used to it
how do you respond
how do you figure things out
how do you do
how do you live

USED TO

I used to be me but now I'm free
I used to please everybody but who cares
I used to skate but got too many vertigo concussions
I used to sprain my ankle but still always do
I used to go out a lot but now I'm a hermit
I used to care about working but have to forever
I used to be very horny but can't stop that
I used to have a landline but now it's a stupid cellphone
I used to be very outgoing but it remains
I used to print books but now we're broke
I used to be a voracious reader but now skim
I used to go to bookstores but now it's the free public library
I used to cut everyone's hair for beer but don't anymore
I used to build ramps but handsaws were scary
I used to have long blonde hair but now suffer a widow's peak
I used to have a license but it expired in 2002
I used to think I was tough but really just sensitive
I used to wear gold watches but that turned into gold rings
I used to paint my nails black but switched to another polish
I used to be a lot of things but still am

INHALE AT WILL

In my luxury space balloon
Enough terrain to ensure a lifetime of glory
Cheap nicotine and screaming urethane
Awaiting the symphony of destruction
Above the medieval façades
& ancient aqueducts
It feels like a utopian past
Visiting a dystopian future
I finally have my own bathroom
& bidet to wash my face
Everyone the star of their own reality show
Babushkas nimbly walking around
Cigarettes hanging on friendly smiles
Unfazed from alien activity
A feisty bunch of scrappers
A truce is made and you move on
Time to permeate the algorithms

AFOREMENTIONED

I am the albatross
you are the centaur
there are so many serpents
who could represent barbarism
& chaos or a legless poison
Who wants to be wily
treacherous or malicious
I'm thinking of The Rime
of the Ancient Mariner (1798)
circa the albatross
A psychological burden
associated with guilt or shame
They bring luck to seafarers
the curse is said to be
around the neck

GOON SQUAD

Not waving
drowning another
seeking rescue from venture capitalists
who walk San Francisco
flip flops and Patagonia vests
oh, I guess it's "you people"
who don't say hello back
or even look you in the eye
I thought you left due to Covid
or no more avocado toast
Now back raising prices
& catching your tour bus to work
you can find me anytime
at Golden Gate and Fillmore
y'all don't walk round there
everyone is so hood
& nice

CLEO

A royal diadem
at the Altis museum
Ptolemaic Kingdom of Egypt
your first language was Kione Greek
mine was Cajun but I can't understand
Ptolemy XII Auletes
after your orders Julius
was assassinated
I can't remember, is your name
derived from Kleopátra (Κλεοπάτρα)
meaning "glory of her father"
Alexander the Great's sister's
Cleopatra of Macedonia
Cleopatra Alcyone
or is it Thea Philopator
come serve me
on the entrance to your
Rome scene Elizabeth

FARMER

What's it gotta
do with anything, writing
on my body again
I'm dreaming about Frances
& ice tub therapy
all the terrible things
she became John to me
Nirvana's song, okay
all of your films
the book is what did me
the first poem in my new book
is your name
I love you so much
you kept surviving
lived it out

INSIGNIFACNT OTHERS

Separated
by a small curtain
standing around
in an arena teeming
with light and crowd noise
I smile a little smile
then back off
from being dumb or embarrassed
I bop extra hard
in my ridiculous aqua cardigan
my hair is dyed
a mop of it obscures my face

VERISIMILITUDE

Content
with half knowledge
ceasing to extract
it's a high appetite
of unexpected endorsements
reading about Kierkegaard
I feel illuminated
& magnificent, extraordinaire
am I a nun turned psychic
capable of being
in uncertainties
caught from the Penetralium
of mystery

SALVO

Of sound
catapulting everyone
in this carnivorous barn
down with the crown
sarcastically the hit
a disdain for commercial success
communique is effortless
flailing with precise abandon
I can't connect the dots
it's not showmanship
just a geeker stunt
all agog and aglow

CALLING CARD

I rely on accidents
trying to explain
I don't care about
what you wear
I'm still a kid
trapped in an older body
I don't know what to do I just do it
I got a widow's peak, beanie and great nails
I'm also at 155. 5 11 1/2
I think this an ad of some sort
I'm only being honest, sorry
Like I hope you are
I'm not gonna show you the map
I'll tell you once

PENDULOUS

Self-servient
vampires, poets licking
their own blood
we all come after each other
with an open wound
the most luxurious
eros I already live

TELL ME

Don't snitch
on the dead

they keep coming
from hosts of others

the open mouth
is a tomb

the tongue
can't stay still

INK

That damn ring
already turning my finger green
they charged tax
on the streets
I feel like Liberace or Rbt Duncan
or Kurt Cobain
when I look at my hands
& make something
I watch the rings
write in red

VIA

I broke
two of my nails

on a stupid beer can
what, you seriously

on the concourse
obviously doing nothing

I have to pay for it
I catch you at every sip

& don't say shit
come off it

do something
for someone else, it's amazing

& don't ask back
bad form

UNDER WHICH

The books
look drippy

who are you
I'm not sure

I miss you
I miss me too

I don't have
anything important

to say. Your teeth
& eyes are perfection

put me back into
your skeleton

HINDSIGHT

See you
yesterday
a proverbial cry with a prospect
of demise
it's not showmanship
I can hurt myself
before you can
the bath towels are too small
excuse my knuckles
isn't blood amazing
I'm just looking at it
it's not mine
so bright in sunlight

WHAT TO DO

Steal lines
oratorically

keep them up
what you're not

they do. Lay it
on me, I want

to find out
same as you

NEW CONVERT

Sized up
by the visitor
I sell myself to you
as a child of the temple
we go communal
& run it all night
when I get what I want
I never want
it again

NON SEQUITUR

You have
to be malleable
& survive this business
Turn it on any time
conversation is everything
How to make deals
what's your deal?
I have no idea
the further I move, the further
I have to come back
Let's run it
non-dualistic

VERY VIBRANT

We all live it
some more outstanding
In particular times
I see Mardi Gras colors
& jump the barb wire
to pick mushrooms
when your bones grow they hurt
like getting shot
by rock salt

PROPRIETARY

Working
with shadows
or a sonic snapshot
braiding lines
distorted
into being them

FANZINE HOOKS

Seriously
you caught a foto
pay me, who cares
send some copies
I forgot your number
hit me up
I've been doing this forever
Logan tells me
about hooks
they are a memorable
melody but a lyric
or drum beat
even a sample can also
be a hook

SUNBEAMERS

I have angels
tattooed all over my body
they're for protection
also a huge pirate ship
the ribs hurt like wasp stings
my skin is allergic to the sun
I try but only get burned
scream about it all you want
I am half way thru a thing and being
I have to wear sunglasses
I die every night
occupation psychic and groupie
my wife has sun in her name
stop trying to get
all erroneous

KERFUFFLE

Toxicology strokes
time to find places less travelled
voyeuristic cold souls
uncomfortable places make it more alive
what an exceptional group of assholes
I don't know these transfers
everything is plausible
when you're a surrogate of others
I allow you to think for me
then play it off, that's where
rehearsals turn up

IN CAHOOTS

Even so
or not so, remorse

drips from you
keep quiet

all fingers point back
protect your interests

blood money
wins out. I'm only

a messenger
when the handcuffs

are tight, get out
spit and skinny wrists

C'MON

Fazed out
I stir because ya already know
give it up for tha record
do they play tha mandolin
ask questions
& make up their answers
Go da hell off
real quick like
go play chat roulette elsewhere
what runs what
we live thru together
smells like strange presences

IST

Overindulgent
what a fine damn
gentleman

go take a thousand hikes
I'll catch you
in better pleather

PARALLES

I don't know
what goes on with it
no questions any side
making too many parallels
you start competing
who likes to lose
unless you like to
I need a new easy friend
the space will dictate
lurching out the prospects
if I catch you coming back
I'm gonna give it to you
dull arms big veins
they really want me
don't hang up on me
just be cordial
I am human too
spirits walk thru me

BLOW DARTS

No signs
of recognition
a catalyst pragmatic
I try to figure what's
going on then don't
scream into me all you want
it's hard to listen to words
I speak them
you burn the paper on the tip
with scotch tape
and insert a needle
make a good funnel
so the dart flies

LIVE TO TELL

What is there to say
it's better to stay silent with so much
obsessive compulsive disorder wins again
how about we try to be loose
& say the same things unmodulated
it's hard to step on lines
in the sidewalk you can't avoid them
they control your emotions
turning water on and off
to catch the right thought gets exhausting
I've been doing this pre-teenage
looking out the blinds
at street lamps
swallowing with timing

FIRST DIBS

The need
to accentuate or embellish
is involuntary
the stories make themselves
give me a Leonard Cohen afterworld
all apologies you go first
I like a hard ramp
transitions get super scary
if you snake me
I'm gonna snake you

ASK AGAIN

Inquisitive unquestionable
always feeling so much who cares how it tastes
my mouth gets lonely too
save some for someone else
you smell sour like me
let's have a car party and forget about it
I spoke into his eyes, we died
roaming a long time ago. It's the feel
how to use, please don't tell me
I can use myself or you

RIP GRIP

Upturning tides
step back and grab the tail
I sign unnamed night manager
flip it upside down
your number is coming up
playing catch up with second hand smoke
different alloys speed the bloodstream
put coke on the ramp then total the can
it's a weird clarity, jewelry section on 24 Mission
bleeding at security in Mallorca
sleeping on the balcony nothing personal
not your normal citizen showing up maladjusted
ghost riding I gotta dip. Popped
blood vessels I don't wanna shut off
I'm the type they think cray cray

OFF THE PLATE

Gonna come up
the stairs with some soup for two
take that outfit off and show up regular
meaning dress all you want
the outfit shouldn't be more important than food
who cares about Hallmark Thanksgiving
give thanks anyway you can
show up with something or something else
bring some bread

ON BEHALF

Principality
of the matter, repertoire
age together
translationese
serving servants
reading castle soup
believe it barbecue
on Fillmore
some nuance
space coast is pocket
trickery no gas
in warlord tanks
throw it down
no masks

MEMORIA

Mary the Medium
sub normality I have no clue
take advantage, lend an ear
I don't have a gun you do
we passed upon the balustrade
I laughed and shook his hand
after I spit in his face
let's float around and inhale clouds
costumes and props form a biblical name
repressing enthusiasm
geeky subjects, giant milk bottles
what the hell am I saying
I love you better than me

BLURTING OUT

It's all gueses
touching feeling don't think about
I see expanses and infinity
unknown authorship rules
who did I sleep next to last night
you go where the cold wind blows
listening to Led Belly in my dune buggy
the visions are only visions
Rhetorica ad Herennium comes to mind
forget it and change the dial
come back later as a jalopy
fixing the oil and carburetor
internal combustions in the main
metering circuit

WHEEL BITE

Road rash
from road sodas

get up like always
shake it off

stained by blood
of another

hang up those
shoulders. I'm not

afraid but scared
no methodology

exactness occurs
on accident

CONCUSSIONAL

You never
really come back the same
is it paroxysmal positional
vertigo or labyrinthitis. I tend to get dizzy
those two head checks months apart
the marble slam knocked me for a loop
then scorpioning in the dogpatch
fine for a minute, didn't seek treatment
too ridiculously tough
stand up quick and start moving fast
a way to trick pain out

VERT BUTTON

Hit it then quit it
I'm talking about skateboarding
videos not that other shiz
it's not temperamental
definitely mental on the temporary click
out of the old into new
grinding the coping made the sickest sound
if you could get up there
fake a body jar and bail out
surviving rocks to fakie no air
was there really something called a coping saw
I ran it hard, helped build ramps
they were older and crazy
sold acid and called themselves
Southern Metal Posse

GNAR JAR

Couch surfer
tell me what you got
I ain't got no territory
you can call it this or that
it's the trick that needs a name
listen we don't have to play
names. What you got
wanna call I got you too
let's be on each other
you go first

PITCH WINCE

Great nails
farmer wrinkle hands
I come off on all sides
rose gold does us good when holding
bat those lashes
is that lattice work stockings
I'm wearing long johns cut off underneath
you wanna trade
or we can get naked on the couch
& stare at shadows
sidewalks write impersonation tactics
my fingers are skinny and long
let's play underdog again
walk all over me

COMEBACK INN

Finishing
to start all over again
what a bore
I don't hate you
any more than I do now
ride me all you want
I'm trying to climb back
to the miracle of
doing it and doing it again
there's a lot of bodies
reluctantly I am

LOW LIFE HIGH LIFE

Negative royalty
I get pitched you never keep your word
in state of vibration
beer cans on the moon
tell me otherwise perfume apprentice
traveling by night stabbing the dark
not to boast codeine joy juice
metronome timing I channel pain
brush off questions
disinterest in success my demeanor
once you have it you lose it
at a secluded beach nonchalant
what a bleak wishy-washy existence
suspicious angels write crucifixion
disillusioned anatomically sonic
hum back into that small piece of hell
easy enough to manipulate

TRYOUTS

Flashes coincide
focus on six different functionalities
stress insomnia relaxation anxiety concentration meditation
close your eyes see patterns of colors
I have the wrong voltage to demonstrate
missing my appearance the spirits are on high
what an elimination game getting kicked out the last supper
already a local shoo-in, last I get first in the majority
weakest link amateur fashionista
show up dominated at the demo keeping it epic
steal a base strike out try not to fight

FIELD ENERGY

Charlatan con artist
I miss you sorry sucky boyfriend
you don't need to attack like
here's your keys I'm totally out out
don't talk to me don't look at me don't touch me
I mean really wish you'd do
we shouldn't have watched Psycho together
how did I become Norman Bates' dead mother
check the ice chest and feel around
Anthony Perkins is in there or his hand
she loves me like a Pisces
I'm on the cusp of Virgo and Libra
my daughter is Scorpio my wife Leo
the imaginary belt of heavens
most planets are divided into
star groups or signs

PARAPHERNALIA

Is it a witch
like we thot, I'm not popularly
depicted like cloaks
alligator sharpened broomsticks
you gotta stay increased
As one who inquires the dead
Deuteronomy 18: 10-11
soothsayer diviner sorcerer
a guest at consulting ghosts or spirits
stage dive slam dancing
not educated. Unclean
Let's make a book cover
bring over a six pack

SYNONYMS

Symptoms
can't find a ride give a second
fine deal it finely
hard to realize becoming spit
use the ashtray, burn it out
subversive hostile gossip freako
give it all you got go fake queen
I ain't got nuthin on it I love on everything
take it easy stop rushing things
I'm with indifference
talk to me in antonyms

FUTURAMA FUTURESQUE

Disorientation
cookies make unconscious stares
you're invited into experience
where I was who I was what I am who are you
putting on shows phases become also
acoustic tea leaves echo instrumental patterns
what's the purveyor melody braiding
unpredictable unusual slow down
sensory abnormal choruses incorporating
a lot of lore comes to life feeling mediocre
leave a blanket of ash on it

FLORIOGRAPHY

An illusion
of happiness attuned
into vicissitudes the dicentras
viciously edge lord laughing darkly
don't cop out it's the same gambit
smoke screening an infinitesimal
rattling the entourage
what-about-isms beat it goon
inordinately featured
to lampoon the idea
I yearn elsewhere
& highlight absurdity
as a fluff job in my PR makeover
fine, you can be my rehab doll
it's called catharsis
the crux of it all oft-sung
palsy-walsy dahlias
getting ogled I liken to be hapless
call it the Dahlia complex
outrageous, acidly candid
rapid-fire loquacious
drawn into your magnet tar pit
I keep going hermetically
just in spite and fuck you too

ANXIEATIC

Tune it out, tone it down
too disturbing to take literally
blissful blessings damaging
being the least visible member
they call me floral
in the corner of my own universe
I block numbers
& keep the snakes in their farms
to let them feed on themselves
in these new mirrors
I can't tell if they're walking
towards or away. Punk rock
heaven or pathetic debacle
in peak form tear me away
What do you say eh-eh
three pumps of albuterol
fever, vomiting shitting
embarrassed, Michael Wolfe
a la Jim Carrol says
you're my hero

PERFUNCTORY

I gobble
a bunch of something
& sing erratically
a cacophonous dirge
the hijinks amusingly sad
I succumb to the chaos
& bark with caustic sarcasm
in an attempt to salvage
I wake up in the ballroom
is the abyss staring back?
I'm as unfortunate as you
king of sallow and somber
a generic sonic space
of psychoacoustic cues
cocooning the versions
please don't veto
remember us

INVISIBLY BRAGGING

Absolute
last minute quick fix
phonetically at alls
where are you? C'mon
don't make it last this way
the iron gates are gates
they don't have to be
from a lover
one reason not to live here
not my history, not my place
I exist in unchartered territories
they find me first
unknown we love one another
without memory
sacrificial

INFOMERCIAL

Too obvious
fit me into lives
I encourage interpretations
the hit makes me cough and talk a lot
convincingly disingenuous
bring me back to the cocoon
I am the object of adoration
toxic genius worship
squeeze it out of me all you need
the smell of electrolytes
upward saxophone glissando
alienates hysterically to redeem everything
it is a declaration of resignation
to be willfully incinerated
I cherish the blithe bliss
attracting an inevitable coterie
a typical smattering of vulnerability and naivete
if she floats she's not a witch
don't warlock test me
all of the minders are ad-libbed
I'll take your nervous breakdown for you
the phonies of poetry
I'm flush, the king of illiterate

PORTMANTEAU

Other assumptions
who cares, call it like it is
extra vortexes
make me jump in sleep
let's wear heels all day
& compare city sores
lace me up pop Icarus
into the cultural stratosphere we go
embodying opposites
I imbue and intuit upon contact
What's wrong with being other people?
Today I'm a maniacal perfume maker
yesterday a psychological jailbreak
storm cloud disposition
makes me coax to coddle
I'll be your patron martyr
I shouldn't be here, yet I exist

LIVE AT THE PARAMOUNT

Mega galaxies
turn me bright
sure there's a bunch of spite
& territorial pissing
I hold my own
reliving the same demo
there's a lot to say
I protest none too convincingly
& make up things to shake off boring
the pleasure is mine not yours
being disingenuous is easy
you're my favorite inside source
can we do imaginary
interviews in front of the mirror?
Let's take our clothes off
so we can belong together
who cares about being savage
tattoo what you want I won't look
you can't fire me because I quit

IN BURSTS

I don't know how
to be this person, nonsensical
& hellish delivered in bursts
you'll always stink and burn
cheers to the anonymous
interviewee and opaque references
how does one get melodic
or at least memorable
in more chilling terms
give me a break, there's no creative drought
only pages out a phone book
we battle things that piss us off
every poem, every book
let's just split any royalty
what you need I already have thru strife
pick up the pace, hold that head up
no slouching allowed

APPREHENSIONAL

Remove the reverb
& add distortion. Finally realized
I lean on the self-destruct button
consequences forget em
buried in contradictions
tourettes has nothing to do with anything
babbling I have a better attitude
now I'm this imaginary scapegoat
I exaggerate to absurdity
meticulously matching words
the poems are throwaways
we become ubiquitous
I'm just a placeholder for vowels
super hyperactive default mode
hiding in plain sight
deranging the senses
into mini-catastrophies
oh, this is what it looks like

FLAUNTING

If you wouldn't
mind I'd like to...
sorry, confrontation
makes me ashamed
Live thru me
as I won't you
I know nothing about
everything. My Dewy Decimal
mind is a great catalogue
while the inventory gets specific
I can make it abstract
as needed. Are you gonna
drink that? I taste
your lipstick, give me some more
a lot more

ABOUT ABOUT

Generally happy
it goes below neutral real quick
so many problems to fix
as my maw-maw says
hang him out to dry
I hang out with strangers
it's easier than with friends
I change my mind over and over
what is anything about
about has to do so much. Sorry about
I'm looking for a better
operative word. Please be patient
let's call Master P
keep it Bout it Bout it

INSOFAR SOONISH

Uncertain profitability
stupefying the most exquisite
amity packed devotion
all becomes joyous and sweet
broke rich textured foolery
the blessings stack up into accolades
I don't mean to be a worldwide thirst
in the rumors department
I bulge out from the bottom
too busy hurting myself getting clips
inciting riots sponsors be damned
bogus charges continue to thrive
cast out the vectors are uncertain
pull up out of forever
be perma-bummed
jokes on both counts

ALL IN ALL

Just barge it
who cares about the result
dredging the bottoms
happy poems get easy
so do hard ones, they're all hard
you have to live to and thru them
jocks and cops try to beat me up
I hurt myself skateboarding
It's my blood not yours
leaking out of me I did this
to myself you didn't get to
sure downtown at midnight
I carry a knife
meet at the stage or black poles

FRONTSIDE HURRICANES

Let's face it
I woke up knocked out
I pissed everywhere
soaking blood I picked up Philip Whalen
me and Irving Rosenthal
went to see him at the Zen Center
my back tire was flat
Irving was like a miniature Walt Whitman
he told me not to write complicated words
& write the most embarrassing thing possible
clocking miles unchartered
my face was on flyers
I throw away the binoculars
& eat dinner in your commune
I smuggled the weed in
such an idiot again and again
it's just a road rash no scabies
make me your magistrate
self-deprecating heroic
I roast myself and blend in with injuries
on the outskirts I do what it takes
bluff me out, what you got
I'll be the subliminal track

IN AS MUCH

Indifferently inclined
I appear the most I suppose
I'm going to love you regardless
I'm glad that my memory is remote
I'm no good, I'm no good
I can't tell if I'm misunderstood
I'm gonna love you anyhow
I'm tired, I'm tired
I can be okay nothing's right or wrong
I don't like this space
I don't like this poem

ANONYMITY

What are the rules
who cares what are you doing tonight
I guess anything you want
how about how about
what does that mean
I don't know let's make something up
what we got on one another
nothing except sunbeams
I see you before you see me or yourself
I thot we were happening
we are but what's happening

WHAT ABOUT

Take what
you want, the books paintings
paraphernalia are all mine
they're yours too
what can we do, who cares
I love everybody else not myself
what the hell am I trying to say
oops blame Erin Patton
it was so nice to see you today
thanks for letting me wear
your sundress, can we tune
our harps together
where do you stay?

LAID OUT

I ain't got time for it
who does who cares we gotta
figure it out. I sleep on the floor
like George Herms
in the pines in the pines
I shiver the whole night thru
woo-hoo can you try not to lie
you try I die, whoever however
that's for you Evan Kennedy
off the cuff free and fantastic
my type of veins

GOING RATE

Fragility king
scapegoating the concourse
call it how you think it is
on second thot, nah nah
you suck way more than I do
where'd you put the keys
don't play get up out of my hair
don't be sad I can love you too
who cares about all these yesterdays
specially priced for south sores

NIGHTLY

Leave at eleven
pull beanie a little down
flash nails and jewelry
no looks in the eyes
only a turn around
do you wanna sleep over
I can take the couch
Let's listen to Vampire on Titus
come on down off that tree
I can hold the noose
& wash your feet too

TANTRUMS

Evasive ecclesiastical
I've seen enough to eye you
what is it like seems like
a beautiful mess
two likes now three
in the same poem
my tombstone should be gold
vast expansions invite
we know how we do
closed case representing

UNMASTERED

Ecstatic
to see you
I gotta do recon
& hop some fences
I usually squeeze thru
then shine the most
teem the paradigms into heinous acts
leave me alone Demeter
I have to deal with these amniotic
innocent blissful wings
I eat poppies to fall asleep
& forget grief
swarming distortion
coruscating evaporation
barely an acquaintance
determined to release

BAYSIDE

Call the bluff
trounce it out into triumph
capitalist patriarchy sweepstakes
gargantuan out of step
I surrender the loser cardigan
into sophomore hijinks
afford me a chance
or bring me back to the gutter
there's no barometer of quality anymore
sue me for not being commercial
say what you want straight up
I don't one hit wonder it
career complaining what poet
uses the word career? Gross
bogus sources of credential
populate the ego all you need
here's the urine test

MAYBE SOMEDAY

Enterpriseless
I march solo inundated
somehow eventually opposing
you have to tolerate feelings
as the head of my local grange
I slang it persuasively
then plummet the blemishes
with my electric wand
I get pristine pop perfection
& am left out as key qualifier
an anonymous controversy
high and unusual totally erroneous
any vitality is to go against
I do what I feel, not what
I think we know

QUASI SUBSIDIARY

Greedy pushover
spineless bullies clout checking
doggedly dogmatic, impregnably
self-assured, ferociously articulate
able to disavow and silence
The squabble is not with you it's me
let's just cover the track marks
into uncompromising antidotes
to the phony tripe assiduously championed
as a paradox of being
I succumb to the larger nefarious forces
very embarrassing and indulgent

UP IN THE AIR

A live wire
asking to be desensitized
I put on my mannequin wig
& sport a new blouse
everything seems laced
& Mardi Gras. Even when
I blink hard I still see colors
Take of me all you need
I'm just a surrogate
of pretending voices
it's okay I'm used to it
tell me what it is
not how it's like

UP TO LEVELS

There's a question
of sharing arias
verse-chorus-verse
mid-tempo this
is my version of
the Butthole Surfers
mood swings
ingrain the marrow
barely alive
willing to oblige

ONE OF THE VERY

Very accurately
predicted more candy pop
one-dimensional hating on everyone
it's an extension of milk it
rehashing an addiction to your past
catchy synthesized vaguely familiar
ineffably captured
not a meaningful index animatedly
I come from a lot of indifference
doing superseded version
surely somewhere

ALL SORTS

A poke at my own
deification, go ahead
exploit me if you gossip good
I'll take the afterlives
we can sigh eternally
embellishment exaggeration et cetera
marathon phone conversations
I don't claim anything
except being here for upheavals
in the wee hours
we look for nocturnals like us
it's not glib just
uncharacteristically quiet

ANGEL DUST

Mascara stained
in the face of calamity
I come back with decisive pranks
surprise clutches exploit my affection
hush up all that haunting
sprawled out skulk thru the gaggle
persona non grata I step over the police line
unhappy blurs don't scar
the attainment is fleeting celebrity
beloved and blameless
I drink out of my water gun
at the candlelight vigilante
I scream loud to strengthen my vocal chords
not fitting the general mold of society
I wrap my head in tin foil
& hold the hands of strangers
they call me the pied piper

TAPED SPEECHES

Egalitarian
flawed out who cares
no player royalty bang something out
qualities get lost
at the expense of other facets
I'm a loving tirade of vengeful and generous
interjecting my own rejoinders
tweak it out as necessary
hanging out smoking Newports
with the shot caller's sister
what you got what you need
watch out for that parking meter
it's a surveillance system

GRANDE AMBER

Shoot it down
bring me down
I won't be around
as we go up
we go down
I hope to hell
heaven's bell

OUTLIVING

You're crazy
oh well I am too
given the intuitive boundaries
there's no such thing
some of this is for you
an experienced simpleton
typical self-blame
beyond guilty back stage
asshole bouncer talk
to thee we shall slay
oh, okay

IN OTHER WORDS

Your goodbye is my hello
a noose is a noose depending
we're all riffs jammed into song form
famously championed as emasculate
complain and infantilize me
I love to admire and envy
aims are contradictory
oh great already faking it
pretending narcissists
slightly numb to regain enthusiasm
I should have punched the time clock
not the floor

UNADMITTEDLY

Due to a declaration
of despondency I concur on all sides
Is there an opportunity
to be up front? We can talk about it
delete me all you need
I won't be here but I find out
we appreciate things when they're gone
I guess I had it good
people always trying to fight
still watching my back
this might be

THE WANING HOURS

From the pit
of my burning entertain
my nauseous stomach
ready to burn out or fade away
everything is equations
I don't know these fools
they wake you up with a flashlight
three times a night
I'm sorry I feel the same way
what does waning really mean
oh I remember, "The Waning
of the Harvest Moon"

TWICE THE VIBES

Get friendly
then hate each other
get friendly again
hey hey what's up with that
in the sun I feel as one
shut up, don't you need to go
nobody's even at the vigil
oops 2am not 2pm
the amphitheater
sings along obscurely
In the fountains everyone dances
to condom balloons
better qualities keep forthcoming

INSIDE OUT

Magic marker shirts
brings out the total best of me
I don't believe anything you're saying
plus you ain't gotta get all at me
go take a warm bath why not
save what's left on the stove
I'll get at it, domesticity
is my forte. Too much tampering
done got me good
I think I trust the colors
they are me as I am them
a little more bleach we'll be fine

PRETTY MUCH

Far overshadowed
moody and stubborn
that doesn't make me necessarily
annotate the interviewing
my essential blamelessness
a usual diet of nothing
in life as so saith in death
our complexities are not not
what's going on here
nothing much except us
you aurora borealis me too
I'm not really a part of this
love you too, take care
wake up you always do

AT THE LARCHMONT

Mildly inebriated
inherent messages win
by subversion I carry you to my hotel
you vomit everywhere
take the bed I got the floor
my insubstantial body
can't control your pharmaceuticals
you sleep in a silky little dress
& dance all night in Rio de Janeiro
there's no qualms or quarries
I saw you sneak out in the morning
& played passed out
the last time we spoke was twenty years ago
cleaning up the sink and bed

CELIBACY

These annotations
clouding portrayals performing
for those who benefit
an emaciated weakling
shaving my arms wearing
magazine perfume
my fragility has too much
current running thru
by nature I'm shy but outgoing
cut it quick and monitor
I withstand several times
unspoken among fans
what does dissonance do
sew it staple it tape it
don't quote me, this is off record
my privacy isn't the only
casualty of celebrity

ADVANCE CASSETTE

Iconoclastic
speaking to the queen
keen to venture
understandably nobody
the endorphin rush
is rudimentary
I slouch against bricks
unvarnished first take
no exterior motivations
at the behest I don't appeal
largely ignored mastering
relative to what is heard
caveats aside let's be extraordinary
a jagged sense of humor
part of the growth spectrum
inoculated abstract thuggish
my flamboyance is universal
a lack of ornamentation
in step with keeping

RADIO READY

I have the luxury
of ignorance, glancing dismissive
get famous the old-fashioned way
don't preordain me
I handle things on my own
no institutionalized aesthetic
it's a bit galling
anybody can do it this bad
Christian crybaby I can adopt
take my word lump me in
I make a living as a charlatan
if I have an identity yarl let it go
as a means to adapt vocab
I create underground voices
& refuse to cop out
I don't know the music
I do it by sound and friendly
competition in low key spots

DAUNTINGLY

Ambitious
ill-fated expectations
a large entourage
fills the dressing room
plop down and talk
suspiciously surprised
are you not Machiavellian enough
I don't want to but do
watch it flow thru your veins
all these people history
painfully anticlimactic
debauched exemplar
of ecstatic cacophony
look at all this transcendence
I thot I died a long time ago
ask all the cherubs
they raise me up

SPACING OUT

A similar kind
of melancholy disheveled
& approximating I play it cool
in the most ineffable way
no need for exasperation
detoxing the phoniness
I take a chance and get swerved
we talk ferociously easy
before the gawking
ingratiate yourself
here comes the lurid exposé
settle the score delve deeper
into window dressing
smitten by subjectives
I choose not to vanquish
avowed by disdain
I own some then I don't

VICARIOUS CARDIGAN

Feeling what
others feel totally sucks
maybe you do or don't
it's situational to imagine
how other people behave
& attempt to be with them
I always live thru others
we become our own gory chapters
self-sabotaging hardly gung-ho
to my disservice I arrive
unadorned towering jovial
we mock publicity
only because we are
the communique is effortless
let's dissolve into a haze
of mantra chant
& amplified feedback

AFTER ALL

Tranced out
stunt swallowing my prey
carnivorous translucent flowers
crashing symbolic
I'll hurt myself before you
not to be overwhelmingly sheer
as a direct predecessor
I sequester deviation instead
the jackpot isn't a fluke
I'm not a commodity
any more than you. We exemplify
explosions in the sky
& conquer the phenomenal
I don't know who they are
they're just like me and you

MINIMUM HYPE

Don't get it
as much as it seemingly does
we're aware of our reciprocals
take one, take another
I'm only pieces of you and others
you get what you want or never want
lightweight sellout past time
hobby wart never heard of
call me back
my voicemail is in creole

AT THE BEQUEST

Besides
the uncouth
appearance
I can change
you on the spot
do you believe
in atmospherics
they control you
as you control them
you can taste it
the only thing
about tasting is
you keep having to

MISS WORLD

Watch or make
me burn my friends
you want to go in hard show it
I know I'm not the main one
we come from a lineage of strangers
the fare is independency
what you got for trade
I'm up for anything
my stomach hurts
being excited about you
I hope to feel the same way
like you may too

PLURALS

Disorientation
arriving too early wrong day
do you need what it's called
yeah me neither
I refuse to read my poems
black pedals get scary
let's listen to Onyx
& inlay our gold rings with it
I love draping your neck
dirty pretty carefree
we can work up a tizzy boo
make your own groceries
all I got here is this
& you and you and you

UH OH

Dull hearts
swoon tons of darts nice pick-up line
heard it on the bus
change your clothes
pick up the pace and shut up
I'm trying this damn tongue
You smell super sour
what have you been doing?
Working not changing my clothes no showers
that's so disgusting
I know isn't it great to finally
maybe have control
who needs to bathe when
there's magazine perfume
just spray some air freshener on it
You can't even wash the dishes right
I don't eat off the bottom
fine I'll start

GET ME DOWN

This isn't the way
it might seem like it is. Look at me
apparently I came
down this alley for a reason
how about we don't think
about what's going on
let's hold each other and cry
I promise I got you take the noose off
we can compare scars
or laugh and cry at our reflections
it all seems ridiculous at times
we just met and I love you

RECIPROCALITIES

Going thru motions
inundating the beheaded headrests
call it like it is or don't call it
what we mean to say or don't call it
tell me all the fun facts
subjectively speaking I prefer anything other
at least try to keep it jovial
the world sucks but there's a universe
it's hard to find it, it finds you
look at all these beautiful faces
I dumb myself down in front of them
it's okay to cry I always do
mirrors will make you do it
let's go shopping and forget about
what's the synonym for everything?

DAVID'S MORPHINE

Try not to feel it
a little gets more and more and more
dance with me how do we
wander and get lost again
Ozzy screams flying high
I swallow colors and mountains disappear
come on back now, it's time-released
he says give it thirteen
breathe try to eat stick with water
Happy Anniversary Sunnylyn
time for a cab

MAGICK MARKERS

I keep it like I give it
who's happy now please on dat
let me know either way you go
I'll be here until I'm not not
join in if you can
sweat it out silly they're just words
We ain't got nothing on us
spray paint my boy
& write all over me
do you enjoy orchids, maybe one of those
these sharpies super suck
Crayola doesn't work on skin
break out the gun
I tattoo you, you tattoo me
the way it ought to be

FOR REALETH

Dusted again
incarcerated whatevs not really
handcuff bus occasions
why are you sniffling what are you on
I have asthma and allergies
there are trees called ligustrums
they create a lot of pollen
go ahead and get up on off me
don't mistake me for being
I don't want what I do but I do it good
you're on the end of something
I care about you, hope you do too

INUNDATED

You don't
know it then you do or don't
I hate everything and don't and do
Loving everybody gets boringly
I love loving not much pressure
look me in the eye and mean it
there's no hearts here
I see them really far off
try to take care of yourself
it can hurt real good why not
We use words to activate
originated by other means
keep it neutral subliminal pronoun person
I say y'all because that's where
I'm from and where it's at
get up on it

EMMANUEL BAPTIST CHURCH

Aggravated impersonal
dysfunctional hero addicts
who care me too not really so well
who can take out who first
don't act like a jock nothing matters
I already got you on the first whistle
okay nice shorts third base coach
I ain't got shit c'mon with it
tell me what to do I won't listen
especially you, you minister
you're not a "person of God"
give me my headphones back
nice religious career bastard
thanks for telling everyone I'm gay
here's a big black painted
middle fingernail for you
I know it's killing not to taste me

SEEM SEEMINGLY

I show up differently
what unit do you own the scene on
same as yours keep to yours
if it doesn't work come over here
we can figure out things cordially
have we met before or something
oh yeah you threw me
onto the hood of a car in front
of the whole gallery
& rubbed your breasts in my face
skating home later
you were eating pizza with friends
saw me and screamed
with pointed finger, that's him!
They chased me and I never
skated so fast in my life

TAKING A NAP

Tuck it in or pull out
you're decisionally living all over me
I prefer smiles and claw foot bathtubs
sizing you up say who you're with
call me at 1-900 and sing it up
I guess we're dreaming together
wake up I like being next to you
do you mind if I suck your toes
I have no experience except yours

VERIFYING VIVIFY

Innocent shapeshifter
chapter queen okayness
nonsensical transient tramped
train me to say fuck you too
c'mon I only need a place to sleep
burn it backwards make it stay away
In the suicide ward
I watch the guards sleep
unstrapping myself to get my phone
I play Queen Latifa really loud
flirting with the nurse Sarah
I explain I shouldn't be here
thanks for the kiss on the forehead
it's been five hours on Van Ness
release me with a cab voucher
please no police, please

XOXO'D

Inverse rectifying conducive
over-the-arch down player who cares get at it
I only got what you got or gave me
Nice sweater blinking lasher earring heist
let's trade shawls and believe each other
I prefer this over that and this over this
tell me what you want and I'll do it
these wigs are stolen from mannequins
same as my underwear. I think thru you too
do I look beautiful in your dresses
Oh wait! You don't wear dresses
I mean blouses, yeah floral ones

AT ANY COST

Thanks
for committing me into nothingness
what do they say
I make my bed and lie in it
watch your speech friend don't say die or kill
& don't be flamboyant
stop crossing your legs that way
doing your nails buying jewelry
speaking in tongues conjuring
I smell strange presences
gutless above the legal level
violation volition never vehement vengeance
rose white rose red where's your head
right next to yours

TREASURE ISLAND EXPRESS

There is no baby except me
don't tie me down like that be nice
I've been copacetic foreveringly
it's too fluorescent can I have my sunglasses
I don't judge you don't do me
give my notebook back
read all you want try to decipher
I come from erratic unknown sources
We tap into each other
you have to agree and play games
do what thou wilt
call it like it is or don't

ALL UP IN IT

Just released
walking home at 5am
the parrots and crows compete
about attention I never care
who cares about competition
you never win then you do and feel bad
what to do about it all
let it take its own course
follow if you can or bail out to elsewhere
this is so ridiculously didactic sounding
I guess figuring out is taxing
you got a hold on me, got tons on you
let's settle the score
over some rochambeau

WHAT GIVES

Freeingly spastic
supernatural abhorrent species talk
coming in between sideways
pour into me and out of me
I know you're superior, only hanging on here
say how you really like it
I don't care much with nothing
except for everything love you too
they call me Mr. Louisiana, not sure
how to take it, give it and take it

BLANKETED

Snuffed out
cold sweats where's my beanie
here's your stupid police report ticket
taped to a Master P bag of chips I cut out
my hands can be shaky like my dad's
Notice the cutting job
very on point there ain't no phasing
I refuse to be wrapped up but can you
Sarah Sarahs speak to me
we come from the Bible
even tho we don't what's up with it
I'm apparently the sixth minor prophet
what is that?

SO SAITH

Reluctantly what goes
okay not okay maybe so miss world
sunflowers pronounce doll eyes
yeah they really want you I do too
"some day you will ache like I ache"
probably not resiliency has a good hold
trace elements give crystal lattice substitutions
I'm a purple variety of quartz
with impurities and irradiation
who are you what do you do what did you say
thanks for playing the piano on the street
here's a five spot, it's all I got

SORTA LIKE

Indiscriminate macho
not sure if that can exist you do
apparently consequential shirt off screaming stupid
at nothing I appear peacefulness
do at such as such requires
I am in my uniform: flannel sweater
rings new nails beanie and sunglasses
Leave me be nervously I'm fine
carry the dialogue ambient beautiful flame
I'm the last and first bitch in the room
see you soon stitches

DAPPERVILLE

Affectionate
overzealous loseresque
you put me all up in then didn't
a witch which we all thot
I don't hate you for caring
It's my fault for being sensitive toughly
keep on keeping on keeping
not really worried sike eyes
the telepathic portal tells extra
sticking to potions I perpetuate potions
what else is there to do
get it free then don't
& do then don't and do

VAPE HEAVENAL

Attractive impossible noise
somewhere something someone else
I awake a main sequence star
& form my clumps of dust in a stellar nursery
red giants white and red dwarfs
speak to me thru Ursa Major
as the sixth minor prophet
what gives and what doesn't isn't a question
your foggy eyes and crooked teeth
aurora borealis me into ionospheres
we don't have to talk about it
let's just hold hands and laugh

IN AFFECT

Initial incarnations inanimate
pansy division ass hat feather plumes
foamed out with a whiff of rapport
Cardi B I see you as you do me
count cool out down for the count
I don't do soap opera skits
throw me to the dawgs bootleg cassettes
yes indeed give me a shot hustler
dirty left under the bridge voltron
battle cat half dead signing
time to regulate money grip demo king
audio break records sativa goddess
sample me and play it over
you gotta get your I gotta get mine

A LOT OF LORE

Chop it up
above the law young stunner
wizards of rock lordlings
good thangs stone to the bones
we're all in the same gang
fun and dangerous anticipationals
something else fabled otherwise
braiding melodies unusual sensory abnormality
aware as a trope cryptic tragic faker
shut that's totally not true
it's fine and I do dig it
believe me, for realeth

CATCHING UP

We move the way we move
be a chameleon jump out your habitat
that sucks let's keep it
in this vicarious sunflower sutra
thanks for showing up
on the French Quarter railroad tracks
Allen, Sunnylyn and I were 22
the sunflowers were amazing
they made us meet us thru you
"Please Master" is my favorite
I super love that you paid Ted
to edit Clean Asshole Poems
& Smiling Vegetable Songs
Not surprisingly you always come thru
as a poet I hope I do too

VAN NESS

I got to run it out easy
who to talk to why who to convince
trust me I got your first on it
maybe not maybe so you're the boss
tease up on it more and more
nothing really matters
I mean of course it does so forthingly
does that make sense for doing me up
I hid knives from you
& never once called the cops
sleep it off, they don't make em
like me any more

CIGARETTE BURNS

Insufferable suffragette city
I go with what's disposable
in the situations either way is fine
easy to manipulate blank talker
continually like it is illustrious comedy
facetious fatuous fastidious fussy
all these Fs what about face tattoos
forget about it put a different mark on me
let's keep it reciprocal same signs
& sigils. I'm free on the forearms
your legs look clean let's do it
we ran out of Newports
& the ink no longer works

BYZANTIUM

Inebriated shit culture
surviving inevitable secluded chapels
we're all in it get with it
fine take a break in the sun
who cares about Ottoman
it's all a continuum late antiquity lakes
I stroll Fillmore with the ghost
of Jay DeFeo, we speak together a lot
she tells me everything
I had veins that I care about
when you mixed your blood with me
I finally gave up and said yes
living with your unfortunate memories
I'm pissed but gave into out of

HIDING OUT

They stitched up my eyelids
laying on the table I'm still here
breathe on me pissed off fair enuff
insults keep you alive
cooped up tapping into unknowns
give me a bunch put me in all you need
nerd handle I ain't got a system
fine force me but casually
I'm trying to get my weight back
answer up on it
when I talk you disappear

IN A POOL OF BLOOD

I come to my senses
& know what my elements are about
this is what happens with what worlds
affectionate erudite fangs
forever love you Anne
thanks for listening to Madonna with me
in Manhattan, Chicago, San Francisco
Uh-oh Plutonium we "live thru this"
the ankles are not in despair
they call it skateboarding it hurts
you wake up in a pool of blood
it's fun to be dangerous
& do it again and again and again

HEXING ZESTY

Jewelry
wouldn't feel so good If it wasn't for pain
Take that hex back you don't even know how the juju be working
I'll put it up on you real quick-like
My sources are Egyptian, Haitian Creole and Cajun
Gotta temper then go ahead let's temperate
These spirits are from my block
We already been hugging sheets together
You can't see the spray paint in the air? Lemme spell it off.
Give it a couple of blocks
& start running hard. We look out for one another
Ask the streets, they'll tell everything. Idiot
I can't vouch, the way we work
Is done by trading looks, you either know or you don't

SILVICULTURE

Ingratiate the tuning
up in moments I keep it household and petty
somehow domesticated
I'm still a City Bird and erase your verses
Pink horse power all naturale
You know how you walk into a room and they talking about you
If you feel a way I apologize. I love you
Baby keep it calm at least
There's auditory hallucinations around us
I want Sally Jason Lou to be fine
I send a thousand flowers
Bloodstained and thankful

COLD CALL

Come to me
as you would yourself
Let's be each other. You take some of me
I some of you. Who it takes
Just no hush hush okay? Actually that's totally fine
Take anything and read my eyes
I can't but know how to stare you down
When I'm I trouble (never!)
I use various handshake techniques
& a hard look
adhering to demonology

OUT OF POCKET

Every bodies
Impossibly worried. I show up in pillow cases with breathing holes
Announced and giving anything anyone wants
Take it as you please, no money
We trade as we see fit
Cutting hair for cigarettes I don't smoke
Get your own shower and sink
Put some clothes and shoes on and change the toilet paper
No more pajamas and slippers while vaping
Don't even sit at my table this is my spot with no food
I love playing games
It's a question of figuring someone out
Which you can't even
Make sure to water those flowers
I'm not trying to play guard while you watch movies
You can hear the footsteps and see the flash lights

PROOF OF CONCEPT

Colossal allocations
Make it uneasy to breath. Fine attack me
I'll get up on you later
When you see me in the dark
It'll be too late. Tell me how you want to die
Please don't be stressed about it
See that lady in the wheelchair
She's got a contract on you
Do you want to live? Let me know
& I'll figure out a deal. That's what I do
I don't charge money
Just a handshake and good a shivering look

BOUT IT BOUT IT

Ha. Turns out
I'm deep in embellishment again
Tell me what to do, I won't anymore
It's not that I can't
Somehow I lost the will and determination
25 years of hustling in academia stupidity
Being mistrusted, harassed, teased
I really can't concentrate no more
Everything seems so hard then it's not then it is
When my bones grew it really hurt hard
I threw my body down for skateboarding
As assaholic Jake Phelps said it doesn't
Owe you anything, you owe it

ICING HANDS

Showcasing thresholds
of non-existence particles so what
They're only bruises and small cuts no stiches
Get over it dummy we do it for years and years
You'll heal up quicker than last time
Deform and inform personalities
I'll never fail you then I will then I won't infinity
Take care of yourself unlike me
Can you pass the cold packs
Not those, well fine. Either works
Aether up in the oops done looped
Roll me up on some Scotch Guard
Spray it on my socks

CON/COURTIOUS

Mediocre regularities
increase fumigation options

today I smoked a laced Newport
pretty ridiculous

in a random car on Fillmore
If I didn't have asthma

I'd do it on the regs
I don't know how it seems anymore

A fake apparent sense
of abandonment features keeps me affectively adorned

& provides the opportunity to
correspond with the fragmentation

or lean back into the temptation urges
that require new senses of agency

THE PALATIAL APARTMENTS OF BEING

Obscure to thine own existences
I receive a fantastic postcard from Donald Guravich
& another from New York via Uncle Caples
then a great letter from Lefty Opstedeal
I'm so kept in great company I feel like Frank
In the way that I'm always on the phone
& no one uses a phone besides for media
I super enjoy talking on it which freaks my friends out
I just got a tattoo of a phone booth talking to heels
Oh well, get over it. Can we at least talk?
All this back and forth with no presence
Fine. I'll figure us out as I usually do
Get at me as you can and will do
I'll be here on my George Herms floor
Listening to trash trucks
& checking for new mail that I need to
respond to

BAYSIDE MARIN

Trying to not take pills and find a bed
Trying to walk and find a toilet and something to eat
Trying to escape but being shined at by flashlights
Trying to avoid criminals but they think I'm one of them
Trying to piss the counselors off by encrypting my speech
Trying to be alone but finding a few like me
Trying to be funny and nonchalant and play the game
Trying not to be mad that my obituary was said to be more creative
Trying not to be mad
Trying to please people in service of favors
Trying to find out who's in what to get what I need
Trying not to get hustled and remain lowkey
Trying not to be friendly because it hurts
Trying to just stare into the bay

WAY MORE LUSH

I adorn myself
in imagined selling futures of urgency
of performance I adhere not
don't talk to me like that, my eyeshadow
blushes you down
On the compound I hide with plastic
forks taped to my wrists
under the bed I don't breathe
I bring you food the next day to stay away
We watch movies with fake laughs
Keep it cool and calm
I'll stick you up quick

BLOW CANDLES BURN TAPES

Brain blame
the hooves want more
algorithmically unfriendly
ghost designing the next show off
Here's my flowers because they're yours
wake up dead again
Totally alive I hear every voice
never ignoring I decide to ignore
They come and get me hard
I don't play hard I mean I really can
Try to keep it soft and mellow
All this increasing information
Not a fan I fall back and don't trip out
I love and miss you Joanne
I wish you could see Lorca
But I know Miss Kids is not a fan of kids
However, you did let her play
with your childhood toy
From Santa Barbara in Bolinas
Back to the scene I blow out candles
& try to find our Wonder Woman boombox
Tapes need to be played
I just want Misfits

SOMETIME ALL THE TIME

These things
crack me up because it's legal
while some are still doing time from eighties
pass that pipe and shut up with it
as far as it goes I don't know
hook me up with a quick one to ride it out
I don't even know you but you know me
or let's just say we think we do
at the compound everyone is almost friendly
back in the wild people forget about people
attracted they start insta relationships
then it's gone when you're out
don't get it crooked it's like that for realeth
if you can't see it don't look hear it
the game is the game, play or not
I came I saw, I break the law

BAY BAE

Under no precedence or predetermined notions I arrive unclean, strip searched, interviewed for hours and left in a vacant mansion drugged up and sweating from their pills. I could see the Bay, the ladies helped my weak legs up the stairs as I did them. We are apparently caught up and there's no age difference so we help each other out. Everyone snores. I go into the main room and try to sleep with a pillow on the floor. The drugs are super drowsy but I stay awake to look out for surroundings. Transferred to a new mansion location I watch the closet wood paneling and the Bay. At the nurse's station they say I have the blood pressure of an athlete and I refuse the drugs to get my footing back. I tell them I wake up and do 500 jumping jacks and sit ups, which I do, and wash my face with cold water for thirty minutes. They think I'm a vampire because my temperature is down from the facial cleansing. I start meeting people who are already watching me. I've figured them out pretty much and let them approach me. I stay in my lane and find out about everyone. Erased fingerprints, attempted murder, suicide failure, sex trafficking, all the glorious gore. Character situationesque.. I sit on the white sofa near the nurse's station and learn the show. They find out I'm a poet and everyone swarms thinking I'm famous and I remind them that's it's all false. They name me "wikapedia" and "thesaurus" and sorts. Fine. In my 8am group meeting I make up things about feelings so I say quasi-subsidary. At our anonymous music therapy sessions I trick the basket and make sure mine is always played first. Live to Tell by Madonna and Only God can Judge Me by Tupac. It was themed, what you listen to in the shower and what's your higher power, respectively. Everyone is emotionally gravitating and continue to get at me strange. I get them food, do their clothes, while trying to stay away. Sicilian Peter teaches me how to make ghetto cheesecake and we become super tight. Same with triple OGs Vinnie and Cory. Someone beforehand drew penises and hid them around the compound. I almost won but Vinnie got me as he had more. We place them in the napkin containers in the mess hall and just laugh. You become friends with who you have to and learn not be too friendly even though you are. There's a lot of pain from others and you have to support them. They always want to sleep with you. It's okay to have an easy flirtation if needed but watch your back, it's usually watching you while you're talking.

HIGH RISE

Immaculate on accident
read my espionage repertoire
It doesn't hurt really that bad
they come to get you and you escape
that's the great thing about skyscrapers
they're supposed to scrape the sky
& you can hide out in clouds
I tend to keep it cirrostratus
any condensation count me in
being high is fantastic
such a long way down I automatically
count the stairs as I walk them
the fountains drip all over me
the water feels lovingly
time to unnotice and shape up
all these colors mix in and out
I am all of them and none

BENICIA SMILES

They like me as I do them
I'm appreciatively concerned so stick me and don't try hard
The nervous system gets interrupted
By inappropriate clauses you blame and I stay silent
Beat me up tie me up shut me up
I can stay silent or be very vocal
Fine infiltrated we keep you up, you up
Talk to me tomorrow
& shut up in it

OOPSATORY RETREATS

In the sanctuary
of subliminal lives where everyone attacks
what can one do but hang back
sorry you turned out to be a breeder
it's gonna be rough and rougher
unpredictably cautious and unsure
take care of them and yourself
make that money, and be super kind
don't let the mind get in the way
I'll always love you but don't cross me like that
ask around, the rumors are true
It ain't twisted like that
I can be your bestie then hate you on a minute
keep it respectful which means
being trill even if you don't mean it

COLD PRANKING

Kick it out
otherwise or not
Don't show me how to do it
I already know way before
show me your newfound enthusiasm
I listen but will not conform
to blanket visions where I pick up the slack
go back to your replace
slam dancing the language
we pick up where we left off
talk to me hard I don't care
we love each other being violent
we're not but we are violet
I love you

OTHER SECONDS

Taste my thoughts
Spit it back up in the caskets
I do exactly what I say or you same
Colossally speaking keep it coup
Feel me or don't feel me
Keeping it lit this or thatta way
What you got on it otherwise then you don't
If you don't love me somebody else will
It's all French braids, gold and platinum
Being comfortable can't exist all the time
Stay scattered or embarrassingly so
In the equestrian position
I stay awake and levitate into everything
It's great to be a part of chaos
some people love it, some don't

I GOT FIVE ON IT

Iconoclastically present
Awareness aloof everywhere
Sure things are hideously hidden
In socks, beanies, you name it
That's called secret representationalism
Ever tried it? Everybody has and does
I'll Hyde and Jekyll for fun ops
Try to figure out all you want
Keep it clean and mean
Positively or posthumously speaking
I come from infinite and descended angels
Speak their talk walk their walk
I am you as you are me as we are them
We're all friends

ALL AGOG

Held aloft
in mausoleum triumph
don't scream and kick me in the face
I'm just on the sofa
reading Hollywood biographies
now I can't move my thumb and typing hurts
I go into the office, paint my nails
& try not to cry. The pain hurts
as it's supposed to. Everybody and strangers
need something
I attend to all the exhausting needs
continuing to do so playing it off hard
I do this so great
I walk to the panhandle
& do stupid workouts like a jock
then back to the same reality
how can I serve you?

UNCLE CHARLIE

Do me up joyous oblivion plenty
permissive to tolerate lined up with localities
Witch effigy is off the charts now
Neither here or there I'm here
Uncle Charlie hang in sensitive silent orator
I'm laying in the bed with you
You speak to me with so much introspection and kindness
Always a weirdo you never cared
I tried to play it off and it didn't matter none
So inviting you and Uncle Ted
In dual recliners watching football drinking beers
Or fishing with Ted when a bee landed
In his beer and stung him on his tongue
The sticks hurt but they sure are funny

UNSUSALLY USUAL

Gameish expansionism
is a long-term trend profit determined
by an unsustainable dept
the framework claims to be bipartisan
unhyphenated or hyphenated keep it hyphy
debt load is eroding as the numbers fluctuate
it's all executive orders limited by fake teeth
the house can't pass anything with sixty
look from trims and reconciliation
the budget is the budget
you don't pass reconciliation
you get rid of it improperly
the caps come in high watch for it
regulatory bodies fake new measures

ON OCCASION

Accusatory
situational aspects
everything comes and goes
& comes back "for the punk shit
for the thug shit"
I'll meet you where you at
if you're at at
I don't tell and keep it to the grave
do as you need or want
beanie backlash
can't be watched every time
I got the fronts and sides
this thing so Gangstar
rest in peace, I ain't like this
but do as my true friends know
thanks for the compliment on my stylistics
& for your curiosity
where are you
just wandering wondering

THE UNS

Unfortunate otherwise
overthinking unnecessary business moves
I move in my own Alien Lanes
I should do when I want
All y'all ungratefully speeding along
keep mapping out the untils
Undereducated I go against my will
& keep it underground as ever
Unattractive is what we do
Unpublished who cares make your own
Unwillingly I have a crush on you
Unforeseen we don't care and keep on crushing
Unlikely never to give up ever
Undone does undone and trick undones
You win it all if you want
See you before you see me

GAME GAME

Inquisatory
evil beautifica lay me down
tauntingly until I'm relax sacred
make it sting and burn
flush it in and out give me more
bring me to absolute elsewhere
be as hard as you need
I know you know I'm known
give me your best best
it hurts so good I won't give up
really, like that, okay
you wear me out as I do you
what's going on
I see colors and mixing faces
you bite me and spit
my blood into my face
I laugh and do it to you too

MOON FLASK

I arrive zero dollars
the streets are free to enter
a sense of inevitably
probably a Venini, probably
of atelier lampwork
this decanter molded
as a flux to cure
my handwriting finally back
hiding in the bathroom
irreversible deterioration
miniscule crizzling
sturdy green of a finer sort
beakers, pitchers, tankards
cristallo glass black chandeliers
a garden of mercury balls
the Swedish Nightingale Vase
diamond daisy trail of tears
pocket bottles dip hinged molds
around the statement
burn some sage

CHAGRIN'D

Chanting le usual mantra
Lifted in the holy braille love is the answer
You gotta let it go playing mind games
Absolute elsewhere yes is the answer
Raising the spirits doing the rituals
All caught up in the pantry
Embarrassed unable to get up
Laying here thinking really really
My wife undresses me
I find a pillow and Saints blanket
Sleep on the floor like my dad and George Herms
Try not to bother anyone
Listen to the Fulton 5 drive by

SPLICING TAPE

Yes indeed
proper verses pieced together
come get down with differences
who are you who am I
take the language and make a new vocabulary
in the trenches get trenched and tranced
not necessarily neccisitude
I hurt everyone around me so what
be kind and forgiving don't forget
I love you or used to still do love me nots
take this one or that one
order it all then destroy
by facials, words, feelings, temper
mind games never get old

SUITCASE OF MEMORIES

There are no rules is the rule
violet pastorals making boats in ditches
catching crawfish avoiding snakes
surfing in the front yard stacking sandbags
playing war with dirt globs fighting already
dogs biting you allergic all the time
I watch me die inside get back up cut hair
delated egos send me wigs
moonwalking provocateur often wrong
always a spectacle double take me
the parking lot of Lafayette music
skipping church listening to Suicidal Tendencies
getting broken up with again
asleep alone in the movie theatre
getting touched by an usher

GONE GONE

Insidious actuality
otherwise becoming some place else
what gives who cares I get it and dig it
elsewise timewardly speaking
I hear the music but can't play it
get at me all you yesteryears
everything's my fault
I don't mean to harm you by harming me
active is as active does
what a bored blanket statement
take another hike or sleep it off
do some sit ups and memorize Joanne
yours presently as ever as ever

CRAYOLA

Invariantly
closing in the come ups get way stronger
walking the Bay say to say
I'm so sorry then I'm not, your fault
I'll just listen to behoove you
playing with blood is so easy
count me in court me out I'm still here
Fillmore to feel more you know who you're talking to
trick me beat me it doesn't matter
find me reading on a bench city forest
there's so many colors to deal with
I prefer turquoise over anything

INSOFAR

Cast couching praying not on tape
talk me out favor favorite pastor unaware of being watched
brother love playing up games
if you don't wanna do something I got you already
surrounding the trail baby oil poison
when the Saints come marching in
Get at me all you need I'm not available clown
rush up on someone else you ain't like that
I don't fight but can jail it up
who cares somewhere everywhere
Let's lay together let's hold each other
It doesn't have to be anything at all
Can we just talk all along
don't ghost c'mon now, where you at?

COLD PRANKING

Introspective
nonchalance subconsciously charmed
flattery is the game
what's your name? Kick it out
Don't show me how to do it
I already know way before
show me that newfound enthusiasm
I listen but will not conform
to blanket visions where I pick up the slack
go back to your replace
slam dancing the language
we pick up where we left off
talk to me hard I don't care
we love each other being violent
we're not but we are violet
I love you

FAUX EROS

Seriously, I just rushed out. I can't lie, it caught up with quickness, real-like. The faces were super distorted, the mouths and sentences contorted. Everything and everyone were faker than ever. Not really really but you drift it out. To enjoy ridiculousness is to not withstand yourself while experiencing what somebody else is. Do you want to meet around those dark trees over there? There's also an abandoned building blocks back, I'm cool with their stairwells, 13th floor, they still have one, no kidding. There's a couple of old sofas but you have to watch for needles. If you hear a hoo-hoo don't look unless you're with me. That's my call and we use it together to let us know we're watching out for each other. We are own surveillance. Speaking of veils, you better wear one, fashionable or not. I run with hoodies and lace and gold chains, wrists, rings, and necks. You can sell em while you're flossing. I never sell onyx because I love onyx embedded in the jewelry and speaks to your body. Give me a bit of time with all these slivers, it can take a few seconds recommending everyone. All I say is that I got you, all the way thru. As far as poets, stay away from them, they're vampiric as John Wieners says. We'll not everybody but a lot of them. Just be nice and lovingly and not backstabbing and secretly malicious. We can all see and feel the want of attention played out for subservient means. You don't mean to do anything to anyone but you do it all the time. You don't even write but have publishers and we have to watch and appreciate your continuing flaunting faux.

GETTING VALIDATED

Comfort zones
Blast the features of front crooks to blunt
I like to get eyes on things
To make sure what I wanna do is doable
Atmospherics demolish my perspectivity nuances
The heat index is off the charts
Holding on for dear life I keep in the kinks
Waxing the hell out of rails for different dynamics
I always go faster and try to hold on
A little sketchy in the middle
So I slip out and get dapped
Too much fire that we can all ignite
A fun time of antics one can't ignore

PROFUSELY

Profusely
misunderstood
Love all you want hate you too
punch me
bite me lick me here's your keys
no surprises
you look great acting out
bruise me again get off my neck
I rewind a cold tub
Flowers everywhere
Taste me or don't
Trick to have nothing on
Neither do I stop counting fool

SO SAITH YE

Unconfrontational
present awareness aloof futuristic
sure there's things hidden
in beanies and socks
that's called secret representation
Every tried it? Everybody has
I'll Hyde and Jekyll it for fun
Try to figure it out all you want
I don't. Keep in clean and mean
positively posthumous
speaking to infinity
I come descended angels
speak their walk talk their talk.
guess what, they know us hard
I am you as you are me
that's the way it is
we're friends, how it's supposed to be

HEY ANNE!

All I see
is unfortunate re-awakenings
which are full of fortune
because you get to rediscover
However or whenever
I like having my back wet with you
waiting to dry laundry
I took a shower once this Gaumonth
I wear expensive perfume
& lather up with body lotion
I paint my nails great and iron my pants
I love when you speak softly
very fast and controlled

SUBTHOT

Suspicious
subconsciously charmed
they arrive to bail you out
the blame self-sabotage
come on now let's be conditional
pop it brand new
don't fall down them stairs again
it doesn't hurt much
it's fun you just gotta luck out
know how to slam
new lips

THE PALMS

Arecaceae drape
the sidewalks pick it up slam it
over your back
just like county shut up when coughed
I see them before they see me
natural causes artificial going ons
on the ferry Hart Craneisms ferry up
I don't jump because I'm not there
It's all one dream. I try to read
my palms but am frightened by their lines
so much embroidery
just like us, kind of like you

LIVE AT THE METRO

Yelling
all the time hurling
noise embarrassed
to gouge away
good luck please be easy
I sit on the sofa
legs crossed super bummed
Looking the dealer
in the eyes I wish I could die too
please please be nice
Last time. I am you
as you are me
calm down we're supposed
to be free

WATCH ME JUMP START

Watch me
pop your clutch just push
Turn it all turn you out
inconspicuous nameless invisibility
I play you on the spot
chump changing on the yards
One, two, Freddy's coming for you
you can't wake up, I'm your boyfriend now
don't worry about the bars
Sorry I thought about this popping your clutch
you need air in your tires
probably an oil change or transmission
This jalopy lives don't give it up!
designed conversation they keep you

ANONYMITY

Richly institutionalized
Sanitarium situational circumstances
Teach me how to burn off my fingerprints
Show me how to choke out I would never
Take my blood pressure teach me to remain
All these criminals and hustlers and feelers
Show me how to garden and laugh at the ridiculous
We make up new slang terms every morning
They identify inmate behavior
We also make our own food from scraps
Everybody is jealous so we stay low key and watch out
The cooler newcomers get a shared room
& access to food. You gotta know
The head chef makes friends with everyone
Stay nonchalant know who's known

PRECIPITATION

Lather up sucker
skin apparently the largest organ
a guest of sores let's lick our scabs
wear sweaters to cover up apply medicine
anytime kisses at bequest beanie queen
change socks torn boxers inside out
who cares maybe a handful
shooting my drone blaster by throwing rocks
on video from freak outs
I get subpoenaed for writing poetry
Poesis blackout cinquain deceased
insensate figures endowed with power of speech
Graphology redacted macabre
fascination granted and served

WHATEVS

However I do is all for you
paint me kick me bite me out
that's so funny who cares
what's on the chopping block
besides free side glances
fine call me dirty in my tube top
these leotards totally suck
it's okay ripped fishnets look better
when you give it up I hug it up
bounce around ya heard me big timer
the sunshine bores
the daylights out of me

CONNOISSEURSHIP

Irresponsible joy
recycling moods inhaled surreal
what ifs all heart sensitive aloof
picked up maddening static
detained by a friendly hand
laughing and sinking into the most
luxurious eros. What a show off
yawing at the police
A charmed suddenness always talking
alone in the quasi I am unable
to be sad. You make me believe
I embarrass myself and go to bed early
all these souls jumping
inside and out. I am not asleep
I am only emerging
my broken mask invisible
with a subtle task

GREEN SEALING WAX

Accidentally
exhumed only to be reburied
for the proverbial lurch
I inhabit infamous plazas
of yore I never mind
just keep the urgings
all my particulars
outsourced for another economy
In this new orphan castle
I endure all the kindly keeps
& unceasing hums
my own private fantoms
bareheaded like me
slow the pace
in order of place

CHRONIQUES

Dwelling nods
wrangled into better
sleep novels
a pampered audience applauds
even tho I induce drowsiness
heretofore available forever
what else is there to od
the nasturtiums eager to climb
why did you do that to me?
Welcome to the involuntary
blacklist I never cared for
you put yourself in it as most do
I cared too much so am this
dried blood stamped into versions
I gather the circles and feel inadequate
everybody flouting to nowhere
I miss my friends
& their older versions

LIMBOS

I am not lettered
so speak in parables
A way to reveal or awaken
the contrast to story
unable to grasp and hold on
to make things more
difficult to those not open
Illuminate! Pop the colors!
Intentionally ambiguous
the parables the parables
The sun rises directly
the secrets are thrones
you have access to
they are given, so are you
to be taken and pushed
into directions

MUSHROOM HIEROGLYPHICS

The cusp of the cap
A water lily cake on the pyramids
They don't know what it is
Taxonomically incorrect psilocybin caps
Tap it to make the spores drop then they grow again
The part a blue lotus the Goddess Hathor
The Dendera Temple
A vase there with mushroom figures
Engraved in cow shit
Pick em up eat em on the spot sell them in plastic bags
Make tea with em on pizza
Trip out all fall back as Joanne said
Best with grape kool-aid

ROUGAROU FOR YOU

You want some
Come get it throw currency first
My dividends are made differential
Sure I propose yard sales all day
I don't wanna buy I only need cheat sheets for cheap
Fine let's make a relationship
We now patnahs great
Some get in and out out I'm in in and bout it bout it
I'll see you on the blocc bring your poems
I don't have any except what
Comes thru my way
Maybe I'll see ya on a pirogue
Keep that rougarou up in there
Ain't no time for beasts in these bushes
When I gotta run I run and do it fast

NOTHING NOTING

Nothing scares me anymore
I am numb because of it all
I hang out talk out loud to myself
So many souls hanging around my invisible necklace
They hurt so bad and just want to be talked to not spoken to
I try so hard but they just torture you as family
They show up every night. I love them
While I hate them. They bring up memories
& make me fight with myself
In stupid arguments I win then forget because I am dreaming
I am reminded every morning where I've been
Oh I know, can you help the voices stop
Is it religion, have I read the bible too much?
I always wanna work things out for myself
Tell what to do I won't and do it my way
Is that Frank Sinatra or Usher
They both wrong and so am I

CARRYING A TRANCE

Unearthly otherwise
Maintaining elsewheres what gives
Talk to me like you do in bed or on the streets
It's not pillow talk it's concrete, cement
What do you do with yourself
Tramp around make quick friends for a nite
I don't do what you do but what I do
Mostly stumbling around talking in tongues
Entranced by overwhelming imaginationesque
Sure my awareness is altered I like it that way
A diminished sense of self
& surroundings and reduced emotion
How else to receive poems

MIA VICTORIANA

You run into yourself
what am I or became where are we
right here sweety big mama gonna be back
rest your eyes lemme get the otherside
food is still hot on stove
get some and some water
listen to music and let it flow thru your bloodstream
you can hear the pulses in your wrists
lay down baby be still
I hear em but don't feel em quite yet
they are right next to as am I
why am I wearing all these Victorian gowns
just be still and listen up
they are coming to the left
hard and strong like
no presence required get their voices

GAUTAM

Hitchhiking
finding a hotel jumping from bed
to bed totally slamming each other
waiting for a ride abandoned
in Mississippi so glad we didn't take all that acid
sleeping in closets together
getting arrested (me) for skating in the parking tower
every night, breaking into bubba's fridge
skinny dipping learning tricks
overdosing on shrooms
living together seemingly forever
loving and hating each other
abandoning

WINN-DIXIE

Viciously aside sideways swinger
I speak into your eyes we died along time ago
Still alive we are together just an alternate realm
There's a bunch of them but the candles remain on the altars
Pushing shopping carts of trash in the dark
Being chased by bees you can't see
You pick them up and put them by other graves
Then go sleep in the bathroom after you clean it
Avoid the stocker Cajun types and remember
You're the weirdo skater in Scott Louisiana
With dyed hair and size 45 pants
Hide out in the freezer steal some food
Take out the screens from the faucet to smoke out later
Steal more cigarettes, buff the floors
Listen to Violent Femmes in your car
Then leave work by 9am totally done done
Sleep again on a dead end street

TURNING OUT

Good to rant
It exerts as it asserts
& does what does like we all do
I don't mind I keep the pace as it keeps pacing
My nails suck too caked
I wear new jewelry everyone puts up with me
Multiple lives bantering with Lana Del Ray
Summertime Sadness in my new turquoise hoodie
Give some slack seriously you gonna show up with tight pearls
Learn how to drape a necklace or spray paint your shoes normie
Divine possibilities are everywhere, perfunctory the word
Or staying delusional and love unconditionally
Anxious hours sleepless souls slaughtered
I peak what generates a green darkling
Widowing the yearnings oh gosh golly
We become as they became trying each other out
I live inside of you listening to John Heartfeld
A bonafide sensation phenomenally yours
Herds of imaginary goats all polymaths speak in tongues
Take a stroll and figure it out, just like witches in black masses
The war machines keep turning thanks Ozzy
My tombstone "is it morning or am
I'm still here from yesterday?" Yeah
I'll go with it why the hell not

TAKE A HIKE

Everyone is the same
Boring depressing unenthusiastic messy computerholics
They look the same talk the same
No eye contact ever so importantly egotistical
If I hear the words 'team' and 'platform' again
I blow torch your Patagonia sleeveless ski vest and flip flops
Who wears flip flops or vests in San Francisco?
& stop skipping the line at the Taqueria with your phone order
I was stupid enough to think Covid ran you out
Nope you are back and have breeded
Super gross with expensive avocado toast
Dang I sound so bitchy. You treat us like we robbed you
Go back to the suburbs and your remote work
I still live here before you and way after
Call the cops they don't care, seen me way around

ETHEREAL ATTRIBUTAL

Otherwise otherworldly
come at me as you please. They haven't seen us around
Let's touch up those lashes
you've been crying. You do mine
I'll do yours. I have L'Oreal panorama Paris Black
Maybe we can match
Do you have any bronze makeup for this black eye?
Nothing too caked or radiant
Something that could also cover acne scars
Don't mind all the requests
It's obviously more about you evil beautifica
Look at all these fools
Anyone desperate for a call out good luck
Bashfully intimidating
I'll get drinks darkling, you the drugstore

TOMFOOLERY

"The hours are so long
I don't wanna be here anymore (than you)
frightened by seconds
I sleep on the hardwood floor
it keeps one awake so anxiety dreams stay bayed
working so hard no one noticeably cares
I died alone, a long long time ago
still here ghosting with existence
friendly with everyone unless they slip up
all a facade because something else rules the blood
full of hurt, rejection, pain and paranoia
they do this to me from my multiple masks
who wants to burn in hell anyway
I don't wish upon my frenemies
to be anything close or like me"

YOURS OR THEIRS

Who knows
taking in everyone's aura
is excitingly exhausting. You become other souls
testing them out they start becoming you
particular mannerisms and phrases
are picked up on, you are them
& act like them using their language the same as
you do with me. Not yours, picked up phraseology
embroidered thru everyday life
I don't care what you do. Spend all of me
I came up through religious strife
& nothing for an art fag wierdo
go ahed blame it on me take all the money
I worked for it but it's not mine
because I don't care about currency
& sorry to say neither does anyone else
except those who have or steal it
think about the cousin of death
& defeat sleep everyday
talk to me when you're good

XVII

In as much
Feeling not feeling tragically ironic
I'm immune to physicality, spiritual too
Verbally and unanswered phone calls not so much
Fine I get it, all the emotional counterparts way hard
Jump on my neck strangle me
Bite my chest kick me in the balls in front of friends
With all the theatrics, why am I blamed?
Throwing a tumblr at my head or being thrown against a fence
How do I come out on top? Patience maybe
With the quickness, always the quickness
Everything is supposed to be pure
Until nightlife beefs show up
As a conversationalist we take people's words
& give it back to them. Everyone loves
Hearing their thots said back to them
They don't know it's theirs but love the sound
Of it coming out your mouth

SOME GET TRANSLUCENT

You say you're coming home
But never say when. Ye ole grande swindle
Negotiating an offer of nothingness
Impeccable instincts insufficiently impressionable
Anything goes in the garage of it all
The stewardess offers everything for free
Off the cuff clientele. Asked "where is your mind Micah"
You tell me same place as it ever is
In the cosmos no one bothers except the divine
Simplicity aggressive abandonment factories
The buy-out is don't regret anything stay yourself
Preeminent permanent performance
Onstage I get a nervous breakdown and go cry in the bathroom
The pressure the pressure hiding out again
Transitions, translucent, trans personal
Totally embarrassed trying so hard hard
As ever just as important and not

PLATONICALLY

Poetry, the most magickal
of the arts like skateboarding
It doesn't owe you anything you owe it
To be called upon, to find pleasure in inanimate objects
to find souls on and of the page just like you
& be eternale which is a collaboration forever
To love something or someone so much
because of a mutual understanding of feelings
Plato knew but eros is sore backwards so what
It's all divine never vulgar
I'm in love with so many people
& have learned not to get jealous too much
We all find each other and thru listening
with respect we tend to dreams
always better in and out of love

Micah Ballard, 2013

Micah Ballard is the author of five previous full-length collections of poetry, *Busy Secret* (FMSBW, 2024), *The Michaux Notebook* (FMSBW, 2019), *Afterlives* (Bootstrap Press, 2016), *Waifs and Strays* (City Lights Books, 2011), nominated for a California Book Award, and P*arish Krewes* (Bootstrap Press, 2009), and over a dozen small books, including *Muddy Waters* (State Champs, 2022), *Selected Prose (2008-19)* (Blue Press, 2020), *Daily Vigs* (Bird & Beckett Books, 2019), *Vesper Chimes* (Gas Meter, 2014), *Evangeline Downs* (Ugly Duckling Presse, 2006) and *Negative Capability in the Verse of John Wieners* (2nd edition, Bootstrap Press, 2017). His writing has appeared in *Americana, Bay Poetics, Blue Book, Boog City, Chicago Review, Drunken Boat, The Emerald Tablet, Evidence of the Paranormal, Harriet: The Poetry Foundation, LIT, LiveMag NYC!, MARY: A Journal of New Writing, PEN, The Poetry Project Newsletter, The Recluse, Try!,* and *Vanitas*, among others.

Ballard is originally from Baton Rouge, LA. He attended University of Southwestern Louisiana in Lafayette and received an MA and MFA in Poetics at New College of California in San Francisco where he has lived since 1999. He is married to the poet Sunnylyn Thibodeaux.

THE PAGE POETS SERIES

Number 1
Between First & Second Sleep by Tamsin Spencer Smith

Number 2
The Michaux Notebook by Micah Ballard

Number 3
Sketch of the Artist by Patrick James Dunagan

Number 4
Different Darknesses by Jason Morris

Number 5
Suspension of Mirrors by Mary Julia Klimenko

Number 6
The Rise & Fall of Johnny Volume by Garrett Caples

Number 7
Used with Permission by Charlie Pendergast

Number 8
Deconfliction by Katharine Harer

Number 9
Unlikely Saviors by Stan Stone

Number 10
Beauty Will Be Convulsive by Matt Gonzalez

Number 11
Displacement Geology by Tamsin Spencer Smith

Number 12
The Public Sound by Marina Lazzara

Number 13
Record of Records by Rod Roland

Number 14
Strangers We Have Known by John Briscoe

Number 15
Cutting Teeth by Jesse Holwitz

Number 16
Other Scavengers by Lauren Caldwell

Number 17
Cueonia by Jesse Holwitz

Number 18
In the Museum of Hunting and Nature by Cynthia Randolph

Number 19
A New Species of Color by Tamsin Spencer Smith

Number 20
Busy Secret by Micah Ballard

Number 21
Out of the Blue by Fran Carbonaro

Number 22
Broadway Azaleas by Sunnylyn Thibodeaux

Number 23
War News II by Beau Beausoleil

Number 24
Hailstones by Justin Robinson

Number 25
Exile on Beach Street by Kevin Opstedal

Number 26
Everyday Villanelles by Kevin Arnold

Number 27
Uncollected Poems by Micah Ballard

THE DIVERS COLLECTION

Number 1
Hôtel des Étrangers, poems by Joachim Sartorius translated from German by Scott J. Thompson

Number 2
Making Art, a memoir by Mary Julia Klimenko

Number 3
XISLE, a novel by Tamsin Spencer Smith

Number 4
Famous Dogs of the Civil War, a novel by Ben Dunlap

Number 5
Now Let's See What You're Gonna Do, poetry by Katarina Gogou translated from Greek to English by A.S. with an introduction by Jack Hirschman

Number 6
Sunshine Bell / The Autobiography of a Genius, an annotated edition by Ben Dunlap

Number 7
The Profound M: found photos paired with poems by Tamsin Spencer Smith with an introduction by Matt Gonzalez

Number 8
The Glint in a Fox's Eye & Other Revelations, volume one of a three-part memoir by Ben Dunlap

Number 9
The Origins of Bliss, volume two of a three-part memoir by Ben Dunlap

Number 10
Proud, Open-Eyed and Laughing, volume three of a three-part memoir by Ben Dunlap

Number 11
Esmerelda's Story, a historical novella by Mary Julia Klimenko

Number 12
Private Instigator, a Journey through the Underworld of Disorganized Crime by Steve Vender

Number 13
Dreaming as One, Poetry, Poets and Community in Bolinas, California 1967-1980 by Kevin Opstedal

Number 14
Art Writings: 2008-2024 by Matt Gonzalez

Number 15
Joey Chestnut's America: Politics, Patriotism and the Future of Democracy by William W. Sokoloff

www.ingramcontent.com/pod-product-compliance
Lightning Source LLC
Chambersburg PA
CBHW051648040426
42446CB00009B/1027